oh, touch me there

LOVE SONNETS

Other Poetry by Roger Armbrust

The Aesthetic Astronaut

How to Survive

oh, touch me there

.

LOVE SONNETS

ROGER ARMBRUST

Parkhurst Brothers Publishers
Marion, Michigan

www.parkhurstbrothers.com

Parkhurst Brothers books are distributed to the trade through the Chicago Distribution Center, and may be ordered through Ingram Book Company, Baker & Taylor, Follett Library Resources and other book industry wholesalers. To order from Chicago Distribution Center, phone 1-800-621-2736 or send a fax to 800-621-8476. Copies of this and other Parkhurst Brothers Inc., Publishers titles are available to organizations and corporations for purchase in quantity by contacting Special Sales Department at our home office location, listed on our web site. Manuscript submission guidelines for this publishing company are available at our web site.

Printed in the United States of America

First Edition, 2013

2013 2014 2015 2016   10 9 8 7 6 5 4 3 2 1

Library of Congress Cataloging in Publication Data: [Pending]

ISBN for trade paperback: 978-1-62491-006-7
ISBN for e-book: 978-1-62491-007-4

This book is printed on archival-quality paper that meets requirements of the American National Standard for Information Sciences, Permanence of Paper, Printed Library Materials, ANSI Z39.48-1984.

Cover illustration: Catherine Armbrust @ www.fibrearts.com
Cover hand artwork: Catherine Armbrust, Cadence Firber Arts
Photo of hand art:Joe Johnson
Back cover and page design: Charlie Ross
Acquired for Parkhurst Brothers Inc., Publishers: Ted Parkhurst
112013

For William Packard, caring mentor.
And for her . . .

oh, touch me there

EVIDENCE

Each morning I stand before my full-length
mirror, study my naked skin covered
by your fingerprints, recall gentle strength
in their impressions, how you as lover
alone can cleave them, each shaped like a heart.
These friction ridges of your fingertips,
these engrained tattoos of grace you impart
through passion and care, curve like smiling lips,
or fertile rows of tear trails, mystic maze
of memory inviting my clear eyes
to travel their minute paths, stop and gaze
at their collection, how they fall and rise
throughout me. I sigh, trace their endless rims
of secrets, know only I can see them.

THESIS

Lowering my voice and laying down my
body unstressed beside you—accented
measure of your sigh, your warm, flexing thigh
shivering to my conductor's stroke—head
to foot our pores feel music flow through us,
beyond us. Love, are we not advancing
our species' ageless proposition? Does
our soul's guardian share spirit's dancing,
need more proof than our eyes glancing, glowing?
Could Plato argue with our synthesis:
provocative positions bestowing
such contentious energy, only this—
our earth's ultimate metaphysical
dialectic—could foil death, after all?

COSMIC LATTE

And what shall we conceive of cosmos, love,
now scientists have erased azure from
our sky, finding arrays of beige above
tinged with white like some swirling liquid sum
of espresso and foamed milk? Shall we fear,
lying at night, gazing out at angels'
eyes glistening beyond our atmosphere,
it's illusion? Do asteroids dangle
in self-igniting only to dissolve
as neutral light, their ancient bright cycles
from blue to yellow to flamed red resolved
as pale cosmetic? Let's trade such trifles
as physics for bed—our glowing bodies wed
with spirit, blazing heaven as stars once did.

PARALLEL UNIVERSES

We're together, yet we're not, wandering
shared space in our separate dimensions,
unbeknown to each, how we're squandering
our presence. Love, is it your decision
to avoid this rose I brought you, or do
you just not see it? Do I hold it for
you or me? For us? Silence glaciers through
this room, old words frozen in air, dead spores
looming invisible between us. Has
this become our ultimate ensemble,
separate enclosures destined to pass
but never touching, only resemble
lovers to others' eyes? Always to come
and go, lost stars in the continuum?

SOMETIMES LOVING YOU

turns a prickly burr under the saddle;
sometimes sweat soaking your mane, my hands swept
up in its lather; sometimes my prattle
as you whinny to it, honest thoughts kept
deep beneath your forelock; your stifle flexed
sometimes, tensely awaiting slightest touch;
your loin wincing, rising as if perplexed
when I pat your back; sometimes your gait's such
I must whisper "whoa," or sometimes yell it;
pay attention to your superior
eyes, read their gaze, gauge the reins and tell it's
our exact moment to let go, no spur
or request required as you gallop, thrill
filling us both as we charge the far hill.

FORTUNE COOKIE

I watch your slender fingers crack creamy
crescent's spine, shiny smooth-filed nails of thumb
and forefinger slip out white strip. Free me
of wonder, love. You read, lift sugared crumb
to your tongue, slide back, smile like a model
shooting a cosmetic spot, eyes blue lake
at sunrise. You stay silent. Why not tell
what your future holds? What's lot's psychic take
on life after General Tso and green
tea? Share if this brief fate concerns us two.
I list queries with my gaze. Now you lean
toward me, surrender cool destiny's cue.
Two red-letter typed lines crimp my lips and brow:
Never tell romantic what he wants to know.

DID YOU KNOW

Power of touch when, passing by you reached
out, squeezed my forearm, released it and walked
through the door? It doesn't take much for each
gesture to create a universe. Talk
of weather and I hear an aria
honoring cosmos. No wonder you smile
shyly when I stare, mute hysteria
overwhelming my eyes, their glazing while
you glance at me, wondering where I've gone.
Probably I'm skydiving, falling high,
scanning hurtling earth below, often prone
to wonder where you are, your luscious thighs
crossed like sacred arcs, your mouth a cupped rose.
I miss you now. But that's the way it goes.

MOON AND VENUS

Lately at night I've danced with a ghost. No,
not in dreams as I often do, but on
my living room's soft carpet where she flows
and waits after midnight, sometimes crimson
mist, sometimes sky blue striped by gleaming streaks
of moonlight streaming through closed blinds. I hold
her, and she smiles, whispers, *What do you seek
in life?* How should I answer her? I'm told
to fear ghosts, yet she seems to have enclosed
me long before I was born. What is peace
if not our mystic caress, souls exposed
to the universe's music? At ease
in this cosmic bliss, we sway until dawn.
My arms enfold her long after she's gone.

TAHOE

Lake a smoke-blue ceramic glaze as Pete's
power boat etches cleanly, Frank and Kay
and I at ease as our captain, replete
with knowledge, cites landmarks along shoreway
massed with fir, pine, and rising peaks still tipped
with snow reflecting August morning sun.
We're bound for Emerald Bay, where rippled
cerulean suddenly glows green. One
cedar on a near limestone cliff towers
over us, its crown a vast eagle's nest.
Love, were you here, you'd rejoice at showers
of diamond tiaras flashing in crests
from our bow's wake, its rainbow's dipping sway
like schools of celestial dolphins at play.

REBEKAH

All those years, she had shown up at the well
not knowing the pitcher on her shoulder
one day would meet the test; no way to tell
the weary stranger—who bowed and told her
he was thirsty—had prayed to Jehovah
to send him Isaac's future wife. No way
to reason her sudden running over
to feed him water, or what made her say,
"I'll give your camels drink." She felt his stare
as the animals licked her gentle hand.
Then, before she knew it, he'd moved with care,
clipping a gold ring to her ear, two bands
of heavy gold around her wrist. Above,
early stars broke through clouds: a sign of love.

FIRE FALLING AWAY

What saddens me so about sunset? Fire
falling away can symbolize too much.
Passion fading in old age. Dwindling pyre
darkening open mind. Softening clutch
of your blazing hands following climax.
Flaming hearts simply running out of time.
Love, we've lain together, bodies relaxed
as silk scarves gracing shoulders of Wutai
Shan, watching night cover wavering light,
leaving us to mercy of stars. We've gazed
at Cape Reinga's twilight, gasped in delight
at Tasman Sea's sparkling blood red, amazed
as we whispered in unison, *Let's pray*
these leaping spirits gently lead our way.

APOCALYPSE

I just learned my old love's getting married.
So now the veil is lifted. Why should I
care? A decade's fallen since I carried
her in my arms, watching her wide blue eyes
entranced by fear of dancing. But, oh, she
loved my wit and charm, my poems, my voice
soft as rain, gentle fingers tenderly
sliding along her arm. She made the choice
to leave before I ever knew, then glared
in pained silence when I whispered, *I love
you.* The cab pulled away. The final fare.
Months later, I saw how psychic wars shoved
her out the door. For ten years now, I've prayed
she'd live her deep dreams. Still, I wish she'd stayed.

LIGHTNING BOLTS

Neon skeletons flash dancing, distant
descent from dark-blue cumulonimbus
appearing and disappearing, instant
glances turning ocean surrounding us
to flaming sequins while you and I, love,
tremble on this dock like angels, humble
witnesses to creation, all above
ultra-violent violet—tumble,
rumble and rush of burning thunderheads.
We who came to celebrate sunrise now
know value of kneeling in breathless dread
to gods' clashing egos, our arms somehow
enfolding each other, our pleading chords
prayers of yielding to their exploding swords.

LUISA

Luisa lies sleeping, soft on my chest.
Your Luisa. Who I nearly cover
with both hands. So small. Three months old I'd guess.
Yet her breath matching my breath, like lovers
in rhythm. Earth lovers at peace with earth.
She sings in her sleep: her name and your name.
Too soft to hear, yet so clear. Sings of birth
from your body. Deep from your heart she came
almost without warning. Almost a dream.
I'm almost afraid to touch her smooth skin
lest I tarnish its color of pure cream.
I'm almost tempted to . . . I do pretend
she's ours. Just for tonight, with this soft kiss.
Our Luisa. I smile as I write you this.

OKANAGAN

We have floated the river from its lake
source south, sighting Oliver grape vineyards
then on to Osoyoos, where we forsake
our voyage for shore, offer our regards
to natives as we forge up Anarchist
Mountain to view fertile valley. They smile
and call to us in Salashan. We've kissed
in sunset, held each other, watched curled miles
of water turn to golden current. Love,
shall we stay here and live like ancient ones,
hunt and gather from the land, rise above
our stark greed and waste back home, grow alone
together, nurture one another, try
to conjure peace with chants to starlit sky?

PERIHELION AND APHELION

When I turn far from you, love, I'm somehow
diminished, though mere phantom to your eye,
I'm sure. When I orbit closer, I bow
my head, body spinning with Nijinsky's
grace, honoring your briefest audience,
focus of my eternal ellipse, soul
powerless to stop wandering space, tense
with fear of losing myself, my lone role
in our universe. You understand, I
know: It's not distance deciding seasons
within me. Rather, gentle tilt of my
head and feet in endless dance determines
chill in my chest, my thighs' constant burning,
fingers pressed to wet lips as I'm turning.

3511 TSVETAEVA

Of course, Mars circles between you and Earth
sometimes blocking clear view of home, just as
war always invaded. Even from birth,
your mother—foiled, volatile pianist—
weaned you with constant quarrels. Poetry
often your savior, you survived Moscow
where revolution trapped you, famine preyed
on your flesh and psyche, disemboweled
Irina. Joining Efron in Berlin, you
orbited affairs there and in Paris;
saw him flee to Russia's horrors. Ever true
to roots, you returned, only to perish
by hanging yourself. Now, loved from afar,
your memory glows in this distant star.

MOON ILLUSION

Our eyes, love, fool us yet again. That moon
leaning to kiss Izmet Bay's horizon
seems able to enfold our island soon.
What causes our awe with this cosmic con
game, deception which enthralled ancient
wise men? Aristotle eyed earth's atmosphere.
Ptolemy cited refracted light. Ibn
Al-Haytham blamed the brain. But for us here,
holding one another as Aka—old
Turkey's mother goddess—holds all, our hearts
surely rule this vision. Our spirit, bold
as venerable gods guiding bright carts
through dark heavens, ascends our sacred trance.
We sail celestial seas. Feel the stars dance.

F WORDS

*H*ow do you feel when you two fight? she asks,
studying my body's every move. Dim
light can't hide my fingers flinching, my task
of faking repose. *I leave. Hit the gym,*
I reply. *Fearful?* she prods, not letting
me flee. *Or maybe I take in a film.*
Give her time to find herself. I'm sweating.
Your flights of fantasy. Fatal visions.
Tell me about those. She folds her hands, finds
my eyes. I fumble with the couch pillow.
Sometimes I'm walking a high wire, blind-
folded. I start to fall . . . Legs grow willow.
I can't stand. *Look . . . don't push me down that path!*
She leans back. Whispers, *Let's talk about faith.*

EMPTY ROOM

Not empty at all, really. Your spirit
shakes all walls sometimes, though mostly hovers,
saturates eternal space and soft light
surrounding your chair, our bed, old lovers'
silhouettes suddenly appearing then
vanishing like night fog in wind. Wisping
whispers of the past pause, caress the skin,
lingering an instant, then lost. Slight spring
aroma, surely lavender, signals
your presence and history. How do you
stay and go like this? Once, your ghost enthralled
me as I taught my evening NYU
writing class. I stood cloaked in reveries,
then woke to my stunned students' staring eyes.

KEEPING THE FAITH

I stroll Park Plaza, feeling my ticker
rumble, checking the babes and store prices
when suddenly a shaggy guy, flicker
in his eye like a werewolf, pounces, says,
Jesus loves you, man! My deadpan comeback's
a ruse: *Yes I know, for the bible tells
me so.* His peepers blaze—exploding flak.
Sacrilege! he screams. *Sinner!* I repel
his grab, sweep away through the dull, faithful
shoppers, hearing his rage echo behind
me, past me, filling the concourse. I pull
out my cell phone, call dear you, who reminds
me to meet up at Fair Voltaire's Café.
We'll gorge on fruit smoothies and cheese soufflés.

OCULUS

No, not the ornate godly eye glowing
from atop Rome's Pantheon or Iran's
Hasht Behesht. Cofferings left us bowing
to their architects as we watched sun span
etched frames of sculpted inner domes. Yet what
stays with me, love: that small statue menhir
in Rodez's ancient garden—gray squat
oval stone, grave symbol of Earth mother,
its single eye, simple round incision,
catching glimmers of light like glittering
diamond. I reveled in such a glisten
long ago, shaking hand slipping gold ring
on your steady finger, your diamond eyes
assuring me we're blessed by deities.

LINGERING

Vibration hovering ghostlike after
wind chimes' caresses, echo confusing
me until I recognize your laughter
in its persistent song, still refusing
to leave me after all this ebb and flow
of learning to live without you. Love, you
fled like an erupting geyser. I know
I stood for hours, soaked in warm, mystic blue
of your tears, wondering why I…what pleas
I should have bled. Listen. Wherever you're
lying now, in bed or under shade tree,
I hope you hear this lyric, feel its pure
tremble wisp across soft field of your face,
recalling how I held you, praised your grace.

WHAT I'VE NEVER
FIGURED OUT

The ultimatum handed down from Rome
to Sister Joan at Holy Souls and calm
ol' Father Galvin at my high-school home—
that catechismic chorus meant as balm
for reason: *God always was and always
will be* . . . Even as a kid I could peek
through the second clause's door, paraphrase
forever moving forward—no tipped peak
for hoisting a standard, no finish line.
Yet even now, at sixty-five, I can't
grasp a chasmic beginning, a divine
and seamless dark—endless race so distant
it boasts no start. Love, even you, so wise,
cite limits to deep lenses of your eyes.

OH, TOUCH ME THERE

O*h, touch me there,* you whisper, leading my
hand with your hand, gently as sliding a
rosebud in a vase, your breathing a shy,
slowing breeze, then suddenly aria
of silence, waiting, waiting, flesh feeling
tender flex of my fingertips unfold
your flowing crevice. *Oh, this is healing,*
you sigh, our flamed bodies trembling. *Oh, hold
me like you mean it!* you gasp. *You know I
do,* I moan, startled by my honest tone,
my sudden relief of crying, your cry
joining mine, our torsos and limbs as one
earth exploding into some mesosphere
of grace, my voice pleading, *Oh, touch me there!*

LIGHT

Robert Lowell loved the way Vermeer used
light ("grace of accuracy" he called it),
won Pulitzers with his words, yet abused
alcohol and wives, staggered into fits
of breakdowns. I suppose, like us, he must
have felt undeserving of grace, that too
much light can blind, burn gold talent to rust.
Last night, south of the garden, I told you
how, in new light, we feel at first like blind
Homer, powerless to show how Sungod
blotted out the day, how Windgod divined
the brave warrior off course, to foreign sod
then home again. But hear what Homer says
to help begin his "Odyssey": he prays.

WISTERIA, AUSTRIAN FIELD

From afar, they seem concord grape clusters
clothing body and arms of this enshrined
crucifix—purple racemes' pure luster
a gift of early-morning dew—entwined
vines wrapping Jesus' life-size image with
royal robe, now near indigo. Love, see
how pea-like flowers support ancient myths,
covering all, yet leave sunken face free,
his sad eyes gazing past feathered petals
toward gray clouds slicing azure sky to streaks.
Remember how, in youth, holy medals
adorned our necks, his form glowing? We'd seek
redemption from sin and God's blasting scorn
by touching smooth-etched cheeks, his crown of thorns.

SYMPHONY

Birdsong, wind chimes, wheezed breathing of constant
traffic along North Lookout, blending with
gradual creaks of bedroom walls, distant
chorus of children's calls forming a wreath
joyous on church playground across the street,
and from parking lot below, neighbors' cars
in their ritornello as they repeat
tires' slow crunch of scattered pebbles. We are
captive to this morning harmony, love,
holding each other, sculpture of senses
beneath these old sheets, this bed sacred glove
of our being. Through our long silences
we praise this sonata, its entrancing
our existence, our blazing eyes dancing.

LE CŒUR A SES RAISONS

Blind channel and banshee, with family
of frigate birds scowling loudly, full moon
hiding, then sliding from behind dark lee
of cumulus, and our Fifie—sails soon
to catch rising gale, bend us away past
Isle of Man through crashing, seething Irish
Sea—will test our ageless endurance, vast,
flamed passion for life and bonding, famished
by fear this sad year of loss, lingering
witches of despair howling outside our
dim halls, their scrawny, pale hands fingering
chilled air, urging us to follow, cower
at their feet. Hold tight to me, love. Attend
to stars as I steer through this lashing wind.

NARCISSUS

Lie here with me, love, and hold close to your
eye this daffodil: sunlight's reflection
captured in its petal, veins like ochre
rays grasping for connection—affection's
symbol in constant reaching. Perianth
like a rippling, rising Van Dyke collar
defines all delicate flesh. Hexacanth
stigma stretches like bird talons; pallor
of lance-shaped styles startles each beaded
claw. Now consider how each blossom holds
toxic lycorine. Recall the myth: He'd
expire from self-obsession—uncontrolled
gazing at mirrored image blooming pride—
this flower rising up from where he died.

TAI CHI LOVEMAKING

Pushing hands, I yield to your gentle force,
redirect it, respond to stimuli
of your warm frame, roll back to alter course
of our caress, flesh alert to taiji
song. Waving hands like clouds, holding shoulder
press, relaxing chest and rounding back, you
smile as I match you, watch your eyes, bolder
now. You extend in single whip, then Wu
brush knee, and golden rooster on one leg,
all while prone. Leaning in, my snake creeps down
carries me to you, and I slip past ledge
of your thigh, where all emperors are crowned.
We coil and breathe deep, passion and peace, two
bodies as one, symbol of Taijitu.

OX

No, not musk ox—carrying massive coat
like a charred haystack crowned by gray mangled
wolfskin—letting its mating perfume float
as lethal ether. Nor barely angled
horns of Asian water ox—notched, stretched freight
like dark dragon boats—their bearer wading
through muddy Yangtze while towns celebrate
its fabled fate. But I speak of fading
blue onyx trinket—my personal feng
shui—I place in my bedroom's south corner,
its twin above my front door. And this ring
of sardonyx I display on border
of my nightstand. Surely these, and gold box
filled with fu, bring love this Year of the Ox.

NYC

I don't need to live there anymore. For
a quarter century I took its best
shots to the head, throat, gut, balls, buttocks (or
was that my wallet?), most of all the chest
and its fragile pounding muscle. Listen,
you've never loved till you've paused in Herald
Square at midnight—snow swirling like legions
of lost moths—pressed to a woman who holds
your soul as you move as one, handing your
doggy bag to a shivering homeless
angel, her eyes flinching, then shining pure
light at taste of a lukewarm meal. She blessed
us in her rasping breath, her bony white
hand waving high till we were out of sight.

MOON

Airless furnace and freezer, its near side
a crusted ashtray, far side a molded
cue ball, victim as asteroids collide
through aeons. Still, love, we have enfolded
its soul in our psyches, eyes hypnotized
by its chameleon light portraying one
night some ancient Greek statue's traumatized
face, one night a bright burnt-gold medallion,
its electric reflection a glowing
spine rippling broad back of an ink-black sea.
This night do you see it as I—flowing
dreamlike within blue-white clouds, canopy
a prelude for snow? Chant softly some old
song, love, as I enclose you from the cold.

CLITORIS

Prepuce like a monk's hood or flesh archway
    for your glans—soft, pink chickpea I watch swell
at my tongue-tip touch. Your body gives way
to flinching laughs as, between licks, I tell
you it's Greek for *little hill*, then grows still
as windless willow while I nibble your
labia—supple minora wings fill
my lips, your moisture a chalice's pure
nectar. Love, tell me your desire tonight,
this night of exploding stars, this night gods
create worlds to inhabit with fire. Cite
what gesture pleases you. Oh, merely nod
yes as I dive through you, thriving within
this tidal lagoon where all life begins.

CHULLO

Holding you on this small Central Park hill,
fresh snow surrounding and falling on us
like blessed manna, I imagine stark chill
of high Andes around us, impetus
your llama-wool cap covering sunrise
hair, lined parade of stick-legged vicuña
encircling your head as an ancient prized
Toquepala cave painting. But soon a
white flake caresses your ear flap, and I
follow suit, flurried back to your beauty
rivaling goddess Chasca, though one eye
hides under Chilean weave, my duty
to lift it and view your gaze studying
my frozen beard, our mouths seething smoke rings.

WIND CHIMES

Not near bell bongs I hear early Sundays
from Grace Lutheran across North Lookout,
my neighbor's gift to the universe plays
in earnest (while warped sun shimmers about
red-oak treetops—hovering in its rise
and fall) like a chorus of nuns' caring
call to matins or nocturnes, dear reprise
of some ancient invitation to sing
hymns of praise. Sometimes they stir me from sleep
at dawn, my drowse certain angels surround
me. Oftentimes, lying there, my heart keeps
imagining we're making love, unbound
in a clover field. Sometimes I just stare,
hearing their sacred, inharmonic prayer.

BIRTHDAY PRESENT

My old love's gotten hitched, it seems. Her blog,
dated last Wednesday, sang out, *We're getting
married on Saturday.* Such words could flog
a normal man, crack old scars, bloodletting
of what-might-have-beens. Here's the irony:
Saturday was my birthday. My present
came with her next line: Called matrimony's
approach her life's *grandest weeks.* Can't resent
that, knowing her: courage of a canyon's
tightrope walker. Mind, talent and beauty
to match. Back when she had to abandon
ship, I felt I'd drown, sad captain's duty.
A decade's sailed by. While I still miss her,
I pray she thrives . . . but wish I could kiss her.

TUFF

And so, love, you and I lie here as one,
fused together by blessed, blazing senses,
volcanic eruption of our passion
welded through ages to solid rock, dense
as granite. Like the ancient Servian
rampart in Rome, Cristallo's weathered cliffs,
scaled palisades of columned Minervan
temple, we last. How is this our motif?
Slight and tender as shoots, we still derive
strength from true words and touch, eyes transparent
and bright as crystal. We know our bound lives—
compounds of glass shards, preserved ash fragments.
Yet healing thrives in many ways when we
humans form from earth, longing to breathe free.

ACORN

Sometimes its cupule appears a sculpted
lampshade for a dollhouse, a basket weaved
of overlapped leaves—bracts armored and fed
by weathered ages—or locket conceived
to bear a minute goddess's perfect
breast. Look closely, love, inside this small shell:
how its round wall rises from white to flecked,
faded crimson; tricklings like bloodstains tell
of nature's endless birth. See the squirrel
on the oak branch there, breaking brown nut free
of its casing. How her sharp, sure claws twirl
and clasp the kernel, teeth knifing cleanly
to pale meat. Its smooth, moist substance heralds
a jewel: opal tinged with emerald.

JANE OLIVOR

Sometimes, as I lie in dark listening
to your passion and control surge from heart
and gut, I fear you might explode, taking
me with you. Then suddenly you soothe, smart
and smooth, making me smile, then tears, laughter,
wishing I could hold you; feeling I do.
Back in my Greenwich Village days, after
workweek's slash brought weekend's salve, I'd talk to
Dave who'd interviewed you. He'd smile at loose,
rambling praise, my metaphors of you as
lark, volcano, wounded fawn, phantom muse
guiding to lands I'd never dreamed or passed
in this life. There at Quantum Leap, we two,
at meal's end, always agreed we loved you.

ANNA'S MARCHES

Early on, every major event
seemed destined for March: Kolya's return
from Middle East; his leaving for Abyssin-
ia; and her publishing those yearning
first books, *Evening* and *Rosary*. By
your age called "Anna of all the Russias;"
by my age, she would pay for it dearly.
Early on, those Marches, she didn't write much,
marking poems by day, month, or year.
Then, age 47, she sees Osip's fate,
penning "Voronezh" to record her fear.
Four years after, holding barred prison gates,
she dedicates "Requiem." Later on,
she dies in March, leaving us her poems.

PETRA TOU ROMIOU

Love, we lie together on this atoll
where Aphrodite rose from the first foam,
moonlight glazing our Cerulean shoal
matching this Mediterranean chrome
surrounding us, mirroring our breathing
as it rises and falls, whispering myths
of how passion flamed in men, blood seething
at mere sight of her . . . how this monolith
where she was born blazes when she gazes
upon it. Never a child, she married
and strayed, knew jealousy, laughed at praises
as she danced when Eros and Psyche wed.
Oh, see her swaying there, love, by the stone
column, watching our bodies flow as one.

SHORT RUNS OF LOVE

I've been listening to Sirius late-
night radio—love songs, fifties pop sounds,
sixties rock, slow moves mainly—like sly fate's
shoved me back to my teen days when sad hounds
of loneliness and longing howled down deep,
hidden from full moon but feeling it push
and pull dark bloodstream. Those nights when lust reaped
eternal blaze of earth's gut in your flushed
face and scorched groin, and shame sent you to bruised
knees, praying forgiveness, all while craving
to shatter a mirror or find excuse
to burn down your house…Screw all this raving…
I've been blessed: short runs of love through years saved
me from gallows, gas ovens, early graves.

MORNING BREATH

S omehow last night an ancient skunk stumbled
into my mouth, chose to die there, decayed
and dried flesh and fur coating my humbled
tongue and throat, stench dense enough to dismay
angels. Yet you, stalwart sentry of our
bed, slide your body to me, press your face
next to mine, mouth refusing to cower
as I warn, *My breath's a toxic disgrace.*
Your lips pause, purse, then curve in smile. They part
to whisper, *Mine too.* We kiss, our sure tongues
rolling like young dolphins in sudden, tart
sea of saliva. Torsos follow, plunge
down deep, then lie still. We curl in wreathing,
mute embrace, listening to our breathing.

CYPRESS TREES

Belovéd, why do we care so for them,
how they spread pleated trunks like darkened gowns
at water's surface, rising bodies trim
and poised as goddesses, arms hanging down
in legions of emerald fabric, forms
mirrored by sunlight in rippling, surreal
memory across Lake Bradford? A storm
approaches off to the south. It will steal
all peace from us. Yet we stay on, stubborn
as faithful sun awaiting marauding
thunderheads. Seeming breathless in stillborn
air, we watch each other, eyes applauding
our constant vigil. Through rain we linger,
arms hanging down to our touching fingers.

KATE WOLF

It's as though you mold soft clay with gentle
hands while you speak of coming rain, how it
clears air, cleans skin, covers and then stencils
our bodies with memory of sonnets
and folk songs' caring touch. I still marvel
at how love's never frightened you, lyrics
honest as moistened earth. You feed my starved
soul with a voice so calm, so warm, it tricks
my heart, ending fear. I feel faith survive
even death. I feel your breath against my
ear. I feel your arms . . . I feel . . . My flesh thrives
like satin petals of lilies. My eye
catching rain, blurs at sight of your sculpture's
form. You let me hold it. All life is pure.

A PRIVATE CONVERSATION
WITH THE UNIVERSE

I whisper to the moon I'm lonely. She
smiles and yawns. I sing to stars how I long
for touch. Glittered meter of Pleiades
tells me they hear, signals love for my song.
I call out to spacetime continuum,
asking how long must I wait. Lark sparrow
chirps of patience as sign of faith, vast sum
of dark energy we feel in marrow
each time we close our eyes. I show Euclid
flaked walls of my narrow mind. He measures
their distance, grits his teeth, shakes his great head.
Then points at the earth, breathes in air. *Treasures
surround us*, his glance tells me. I watch him
dance off, humming a hymn to his theorem.

WHEN WE DANCE

When we dance, we touch hands as if fingers
were flower petals, rub cheeks as though bone
below the skin might break. Breathing lingers
in long sighs, anticipates life alone
after music ends. Breasts and bellies press
like praying palms, our flexing thighs glancing
then fleeing as lithe, rhythmic feet caress
the gleaming floor, our diamond eyes dancing,
matching rotating globe's romancing light
above us, symbol of universe's
love for us, for all waltzing through this night
of singing strings, our whispers soft verses
from inspired angels. Their wings surround us,
unseen shields. Flowing hands rise to crown us.

LONELINESS IS A GRAY WOLF

Apex predator, you stalk both species
within me, my calculating brain and
reflexive heart sheared to ragged pieces
by your carnassials' piercing command
once more of my stunned mind and emotion,
your golden-yellow eyes leering pleasure
as I become your sly preying motion,
your howling at twilight, loping to lure
myself away from any lair of hope.
Taking on your body language, I slant
my ears, narrow sad eyes, arch my back, grope
and whimper, yelp in fear, passionate pants
as I expose my vulnerable throat
and underside, its ripped and bloody coat.

TWILIGHTWOMBDAY

I've discovered an eighth day of the week
divided and grafted in the seven
like special cells demanding brain to seek
deep dreams while awake. I fly to heaven,
grovel in hell, float in limbo, manage
to win and lose love through dice games of soul,
unearth great plans to save the world, bless age
rather than fear it, take loving control
of the universe. I'm in the shower
when this day rises amidst the warm mist
of pelting water and steam, the power
of silky lather coating me from wrist
to ankle—skin of new humanity
caressing fantasy and sanity.

STUFF

No, not the generic term ignorant
or lazy humans employ to avoid
specifics. Not base trash nor virgin land,
nor dunk shot by some goliath jock void
of literacy. I ape Confucius
who *would call things by their right names*. Lest my
definition denial confuse us,
I speak of Kidderminster's old woolsey-
linsey cloth—compact warps of linen yarn
and worsted weft British lawyers required
in their courtroom gowns. Where'd you find this darned
relic, love? Its famed industry expired
centuries ago. Oh, judge me in awe.
We lie here: you, clothed queen; I'm in the raw.

CHASMA BOREALE

These red cliffs of Mars fill our telescope's
lens like streams of claret flowing over
pewter. Surely these deep-crimson cords, ropes
like arteries from some passionate heart,
must rise from volcanoes buried beneath
this cap's metallic crust of water-ice—
surface rich as satin fabric bequeathed
by Shakespeare's queen. How your enamored eyes
take in this scene remind me of the night
I surprised you with that Brittania-
metal vase of polyanthuses. Sight
of their coral petals brought mania:
lovemaking beneath our grand piano,
releasing our own buried volcanoes.

SOLAR PROMINENCE

Burning plasma lifts from sun, its two forms
like lithe dancers caught up in passionate
music from eternity. Love, this storm
of space reveals all art, grace incarnate.
How is it you now play Tchaikovsky's great
piano concerto, its turbulent
keys giving way to sardonic cascades,
strings swirling through like excited children
to join the grand dance? How our telescope
captures these massive figures furling and
unfurling through magnetic fields. They grope
in cloudlike curls, powerless to ghosts' hands
controlling their entranced ballet, bodies
like ours in bed: cyclone, yet flawless peace.

HEARTS

Some I've scalpeled skillfully from thorax,
dissected and skewered on silver prongs,
roasted over flames until fibroblasts
grew black, signaling well done. Though I've longed
only to taste excitable cells, I've
settled for the full meals. Some have plagued me
with such passion, I've devoured them live,
severing breastbones with single blows, freed
cardiac muscles with violent rips,
perhaps even swallowing raw flesh whole,
tasting only blood drops licked from my lips,
belching and moaning, *Oh, my damned soul*.
Yet now there's you, love. You stun me, impart
a surgeon's touch: graft my heart to your heart.

HOMECOMING

If you were here, I'd point to the night sky,
cite how the three-quarter moon, lopsided
as some ancient Roman coin, must have spied
you waving last year from that high, crowded
row in War Memorial Stadium,
and returned this evening for your encore.
But you're not here, are you? Among loud drums,
Go Rockets! shouts, crowd currents flowing forth
and back like conscience, I glance from time to
time, thinking I see you between pass plays,
waving down to me as I wave up. Though
I know that's not how life goes, it can't sway
me from past moments composing my tune
of memory. Or so I tell the moon.

LEAF AND HAND

This Northern Red Oak leaf covers my left
palm and fingers, its pigment fading from
forest-green to yellow-green, a bereft
chameleon caught in the act. Right palm comes
beside it as if taking communion
from nature, and I study plant veins and
my veins, its stalk turning to lifeline on
through to leaf's tip, while my rough-edged,
stretched hand's ine arcs from near wrist to base
of index finger and beyond. Love, do you believe
this curved furrow within our aging, flexed
flesh determines our days? Like withered leaves
we fade as the hand curls closed? Do we share
life beyond us, as loving leaves bear air?

AUTUMNAL EQUINOX

It's today, you know. Love, shall we call it
coincidence we lie hear listening
to Neil Diamond sing *Be*—of the poet's
eye and the Sun God making our day? Sing
of sand, stone and bone? The Iranians
celebrate Jashne Mihragan this day,
hearts honoring the divine covenant,
and thus friendship. On tables they display
rose water, apples, and pomegranates,
burn frankincense and sing. Anglo-Saxons
and Celts bowed to *haleg-monath*, this date
its genesis. Now our source, blazing sun,
sails across the equator, impartial
to light or dark. Invites us to love all.

PRAESEPE

Love, see how to the naked eye this star
cluster ignites astronomers' visions.
Eratosthenes, on Cyrene hill far
from Greece, imagined shining manger, on
each side a feeding ass awarded heaven
for bearing Dionysus and Silenus
to defeat Titans. Aratos christened
it Little Mist. Stargazers around us
see a beehive. I view a jeweled face,
glowing points of forehead, cheekbones, and chin,
a moistened glistening—celestial trace
of graceful Alcyone newborn, risen
from the sea. Yes, a new myth I've designed.
Or now reality: Your face divine.

POLAND, EARLY SPRING

We rest under a lone oak. Our tired eyes
follow the Sokolda's narrow, scythe-like
curve—thin river whose genus we'd revise
to creek back home. The tree nests a grey shrike.
You call it a vagrant, too far north. Bass
break the water's surface, large mouths snapping
at minnows. Touching the oak, our thoughts pass
to the ancient Bartek we saw, strapping
as a Cyclops, in the wi tokrzyyskies
near Kielce. You suddenly wince with pain,
recalling gnarled field of spruce carcasses
in the Karkonosze; curse acid rain.
I hold your chilled hand. Study the distant thaw
of pines. Whisper, "Like winter in Arkansas."

I'M WRITING WHILE

Johnny Mathis sings *A Certain Smile*, strings
and sopranos surrounding him, while Nat
King Cole soothes *September Song* to Shearing's
clear ivory keys—raindrops entrechat
through wind chimes—while Sinatra croons *Stardust*,
while Eartha Kitt chanteuses *Smoke Gets In
Your Eyes*, throaty purr of Catwoman just
sipping the milk from a silver bowl when
Mathis returns with *Chances Are*. How would
Li Po respond, do you think, lying by
the Yangtze with iPod, feeling spry wood-
winds caress Eckstine's vibrato softly
over Internet? Drunk, would he still drown,
trying to embrace the moon's reflection?

DENVER AIRPORT AT DUSK

Rockies' peaks form Goliath's ruptured spine
after the fall, their distant silhouette
also his dried-blood lower jaw, divine
images altering with this sunset's
varied moods, seeming to fade behind bold
mountains, then blazing anew, fire mirrored
in vast cloud cluster, furnace to drive cold
from heaven. Now scarlet. Now Persian red.
And now this mammatus canvas recalls
Pillars of Creation—lustered columns
of dust crowning Eagle Nebula—sprawled
across starry space like lava. Solemn
as priest and nun at sunrise, we would gaze
through telescopes, deep breaths our humble praise.

CLEANSING

This water runs across my hands like air
over alveoli's purified beds
of capillaries. This warm water flares,
reflecting light, forming gleaming stream fed
by the hydrogen bond. This bubbling flow
of water, earth's master solvent blending
with alkali and fatty acids, glows
with globes of soapsuds, their clusters mending
my fingers' sins, my palms' reflexive greed,
my angry knuckles' bare, slashing assaults.
This splashing, filmy water seems to plead
for grace, praying my life drains free of fault
as my soft, forgiven grasp enfolds you,
night's rain praising my blessed gift to hold you.

BEAST

Love, you've watched me at my preying levels:
lower vertebrate like shark, my angry
mouth a seething spiracle. I'll grovel
like leech to anesthetize as I try
to swallow you whole. I fear my bête noire,
drowning in black bile, fierce insanity
gazing in mirror, fancying a gar
reciting Hitler—epic vanity.
Yet you, my wise Metis, cunning magic
flowing from your fingertips, encircle
your lithe frame with gleaming steel. No tragic
end. You heal black humor with miracle
of wit. Sing how I'm the good shepherd's lamb
(not the ass of burden we know I am).

QUIVERING SILHOUETTES

This monstera leaf shaped like sea-green heart
    grasps sun through Catherine and Eric's wall
of living-room windows, creating art
of quivering silhouettes on a pall
of golden yellow like a cardiac
X-ray revealing flexing mitral valve
and papillary muscles' last contracts,
or now shaggy felt uterine wall halved
by a single brave sperm, head and long tail
like a twitching bean sprout. And suddenly
I recall candlelit night we regaled
our daughter's conception, eyes silently
deciding to make life, bodies kneeling,
quivering silhouettes on the ceiling.

BELOVÉD

Plato, knowing of guardian angels,
leads Socrates to cite them in *Phaedo*
as guides. Job speaks of go-betweens. Michael
appears in prophet Daniel's book. And so
we stand together again, our bodies
whole and blessed, no doubt led to each other
through these keepers of all humans, at ease
with our softest touch despite vanished years,
our flesh and tears so far from sight. Perhaps
we called upon these nurturing spirits
in our youth, not knowing honesty as
prayer. But patrons know. Let's say they hear it
in our laughter. Surely your grace delights
protectors' eyes, always with God in sight.

LAKE OF STARS

Oh, see how we're double-blessed as night sky
and forest's edge surround Lake Ouachita,
stars and trees holding their vast and trusty
stations while nature reflects its art far
across smooth water's smoke-glass surface. Love,
see how Jupiter's glow, though a dwarfed moon,
still highlights the Milky Way's sequined gloves
both above us and along the shore. Soon
fireflies will try to match this radiance,
their colonies of pale reddish light caught
in the crickets' rhythmic song, swirling dance
of flaming pearls sprinkling the tall pines. What
can we do to share this lustrous surprise?
Ah, yes. I see the answer in your eyes.

GREAT PASSION

And so, Great Passion, I'm now convinced you
never rest, only play sly chameleon,
sometime eruptive prominence—flamed hue
like roiling spirit unfurling from sun—
sometime feigned crescent of peace, like Saturn's
pale reflective surface, Rhea a black
lens occulting its center (how we yearn
to touch it but can't), sometime galactic
distortion like this mirage of blue cloud
circling misty dot of light—a leaping
porpoise curling the moon. How we've all bowed,
feeling as though we've been roused from sleeping,
seeing Namib Desert's towering dunes,
violent winds crowning them with lagoons.

JUPITER OPPOSITION

There at opposition as the sun sets,
Jupiter rises, then falls with solar
ascent. And now I observe our planets—
you and I—how we lift and drop, polar
bodies rarely in sync, lodestones rolling
awry seeking drama not comedy,
war not peace, sacred temple bells tolling
our slow demise. Hear their sad melody?
I don't ask you this aloud. Only hold
you close, monk-silent, watching Jupiter
over Ephesus this full-moon night, cold
pushed away by our caress, junipers
blocking chilling wind here at Hadrian's
temple, its crumbling pillars our omen.

LAVENDER

You know by now Apis mellifera
has deserted you, leaving beekeepers
befuddled and honeyless. But there's a
French chef in Provence who'll gladly reap your
dry buds for Massialot's Crème brûlée.
You helped Magdalene wash the carpenter's
feet. England's virgin queen demanded aides
display your blossoms each day of the year.
I'd say your resumé's solid. How kind
of you to share your scent worldwide through fields
and gardens, balms and perfumes. Now we find
you in potpourris, making the moth yield
when your team's tossed in closets. A borough
woman nurtures your shoot by the window.

DARK SKY OVER
DEATH VALLEY

We drove all scorching day up 190
from near Shoshone to Valley Junction,
rumbled south to Badwater—our country's
lowest point—and now lie here, our unction
this night sky pouring over Panamint
Range, Racetrack Playa's dry basin flowing
beneath us like colonies of veined slits
in an ancient temple's floor, stars glowing . . .
no . . . exploding around us. Love, we may
not see this dark night again, the Milky
Way's arch like a blazing bridge to Yahweh.
The world falls prey to civilized light. See
how that distant strip of horizon's bright:
man's torch burning angels' eyes from our sight.

PENIS ENVY

What's with you? Old days, you played the perfect
gentleman, rising at once when ladies
entered the room, stayed stately and erect
throughout conversation and beyond. Yes,
I recall those special times some fair lass
kept you leaping like Flipper beneath jeans'
zippered surface. One night you showed no class,
eked out your mouse in the movie house. Scenes
of such thrive in our archives. Why can't you
shape up now? Show some control. Cash in on
your stint at the late show. You act like flu's
left you noodle limp. Bring back that passion,
like nights barreling over Niagara.
I hate these fake days, reaching for Viagra.

VAGINA

I touch your vagina, like an iris
unfolding, labia menora's petals
sensing caress of my soft fingertips.
Its tongue awaits my tongue. As I settle,
I taste your vagina, thick moisture from
a hidden spring secreting with each flex
and flinch. Did this nectar help gods become
immortal, its divine flow heaven's text
of revelation? Did Bartholin know
what I now know? Drop his microscope, don
this wet sheath? And so my penis sheathes now,
diving through your vagina, Poseidon
recalling his first great surge as a boy,
swimming in ocean's universal joy.

HOW DEEP IS SADNESS?

Far as earth's core-mantle boundary, its
4,000 degrees Celsius flaming
limit to our agony? Can limits
exist in core's iron-dominated ring,
springing magnetic fields to protect us
from solar storms? Does our solid center,
liquid outer crux somehow reflect us?
Can our reason ever hope to enter
feeling, route its uncharted boundaries
of mountainous wars and low-valleyed peace?
Fair Psyche, confused by the mystery
of her night-veiled lover, made Cupid flee
by lighting the oil lamp. Oh, how she yearned,
walked into hell, not knowing he'd return.

VISIONS, I SEE VISIONS

Sandy Denny, dressed as in tintype, steps
off the album cover and kisses me.
I reach out, softly touch her stretched triceps,
our bodies glowing, pastel comets free
and flowing through Trifid Nebula, dawn
mountains of opaque dust coating us, pale
as angels. Now night here in Washington
Square Park, William Packard leaning on rail
next to me. We watch walkers pass. Poems
brief as breath slip through his lips, their spirits
singing. He grasps the small book, potent rim
of his hand raising it toward the moon, its
pages burning like stars. *Art never ends*,
he whispers. I watch his great form ascend.

SOLSTICE MOONRISE

Temple of Poseidon's pillars clinch wide
in gnarled columns, those silhouetted teeth
some whale skull's only remains. Say it died
when the sea's harsh father rose from beneath
Aegean's waves in rage, lashed the mammoth
mammal against Cape Sounion's vast crest,
leaving it to parch and decay. The mouth
of glowing moon yawns behind these darkest
of ruins, visible only to us
as villagers sleep, and to that sailor
guiding his craft through shimmering stardust
below, his midnight song a drunken prayer:
Artemis, send a new love to adore
me like a god, there on Patroklou's shore.

GLAZE

Not speckles on your sweet holiday ham,
sintered oxide covering metal door,
reflective lens of your digital cam
nor transparent surface of marble floor.
Not vitreous coating on ceramic
vase holding my passion-red rosebud gift,
nor glossy gleam of your blouse's fabric,
but your thin-iced face, love, after our rift:
smooth and lustrous, yet refusing to melt
to my apology, or crack a smile
at my amending joke. I know you felt
my excuse a lie, my intentions vile.
I could tell when your eyes lost their soft glow,
their frost-glistened gaze like frozen windows.

FOGBOW

Out from Ocean Beach, that white, mystic arc
spanning sea like a melting fluorescent
tube appears a rainbow's lost ghost, its stark
absence of color making me repent
failed loves, spent fortunes, selfish wasted hours
lying to people I didn't even
know, diverting sunlight away—not towards
them—like that fogbow's fine mist must prevent
prismic hues from reaching artists' eyes as
they stand on the cliff above us. Tell me,
last night when we said we loved—whispers passed
through darkness in passion and hope—did we
speak the truth or commit a sacrilege,
our vows soon dissolving like that pale bridge?

ANTIHYMN FROM FAR AWAY

And still she rises with you, Great Breather,
within subconscious response of spirit
through lungs and heart's contraction. Like ether,
flammable anesthetic, I fear it
yet welcome it: memory a sleeping
lion dreaming of some future assault.
Good of you, walking with me through weeping,
into brief ravines of peace. *Not your fault*
or hers. Your haunting words resound within,
a decade's echoed lyric. Can't you let
up on me now? Forgive and cast off sin
from our human condition? End regret?
Humbly I bow, one among the faithful.
Shall I lie in prayer, and say I'm grateful?

GROIN

See how its curve captures grains, expanding
beach along this Coronado hotel
front. Its bent length of dark rocks, commanding
every pebble's fate, starves neighbors' portals
ranging south. Better to view Tedesko's
design at St. Louis Airport, groin
vaults like pale arches awaiting frescoes
on a cathedral's cylindrical wings.
Yet without it, we could not lie here, tide
able only to lick our feet, bodies
aroused by warm sand at midnight. You cried
softly when I touched you there, then long sighs
as I caressed your moist curls so lightly,
our muscles wrapped in rhythm with the sea.

SOUL

The smallest particle of a thing. No.
The only thing. Realizing so much
love, it glows. Seethes white hot. Explodes into
every thing. Cells of reason, heat, must touch
and unite. Some form fluid. Some light. Earth.
Us. Within our magnetic fields, when did
fear form, stall rhythm, reverse flow? Pained birth?
Learning of death? Walk through the forest. Sit
by the stream. Gaze out at the canyon. Does
the silent rock know? The rippling water?
Surely that great oak—as endless leaves grow,
the ancient bark having sensed faith, slaughter,
peace, laughter rise from ages of heathen
madness—knows. Shares essence of our breathing.

CHILDSONG

The small girl across the street is screaming.
Not painful cry, but caught in her childsong,
discovering sharp tones beyond dreaming,
delighted in their shrill, startling height, long
as breath will allow, intense with spirit
Ulysses must have known, bound to ship's mast,
craving wisdom beyond death. Love, hear it
in her voice, joy longing to kiss our vast
universe? Can we match it with our mute
choices, sharing life's passion through glances,
smiles, hands and arms latching our resolute
bodies, braving what we see? Faith dances
through us, stirred to heal deep fractures from pain,
leads us to sharing our childsong again.

TO HOLD YOU IN MY MIND

To hold you in my mind like a primrose
petal pressed under glass will just not do.
Better lily in clear pond floating close
as breath to clouds mirrored in water's blue
reflection, as though blessed to float and fly
at once, ultimate life of freedom: What
we've longed for all this time. I can't say why
I sit next to you, watch your motions, chat
one moment, speak heartfelt the next of friends,
family, body, spirit, our constant
thread of honesty curling through. You send
me to a new space, the outer you and
inner you flowing through my sacred door
like light, as though we've done this all before.

WHEN YOU SMILE . . .

. . . you may not realize how Sirius,
brightest of stars (its name Greek for searing),
grows brighter still. How brilliant Canopus—
its flame of white-hot sapphire appearing
in constellation Carina, jewel
of Argo Navis—energized by warm
rush of your glow, explodes: starlight fueled
by your inner sun reflected in charm
of your face. Please don't fear as I tell you
this. Astronomers have sensed for a while
how, somewhere on earth, carbon burns into
neon, just as stars, through one woman's smile.
They've testified in theses this is true,
confessing they don't know who. But I do.

MAKING LOVE TO A GALAXY

Hold me in your spiral arms, massage me
through your hot young stars, their open clusters
scorching my tense pores, hydrogen and he-
lium enfolding my skin in luster
of your disk opaque, swimming in halo's
age-old stars, humming their vibrant soulsongs,
their random elliptical orbits slow
as sea's ebb as my body floats along
toward your nucleus, my being absorbed
in magnetic field of invisible
you: dark matter I may never know, orb
of endless gravitation, forceful pull
passing all I can conceive, conceiving
me in your missing mass, coming, leaving.

LOGARITHMIC SPIRAL

Descartes first described it. Bernoulli called
it a miracle, amazed how it grows
with each curve, but never altars shape. All
you have to do: study nature. You'll know
by soft swirls in sunflowers, nautilus
shells. The moth approaches flame the same way
the hawk falls toward prey. The Coriolis
force affects the cyclone's gyre, doesn't sway
its form. The Milky Way's arms enfold space,
mirror the charming curves of broccoli.
Subatomic particles seem to race
on similar paths of geometry
in bubble chambers. Eye's iris contracts
in quick curls (like toes) when humans climax.

WISDOM

Wisdom . . . can either absorb or destroy us,
depending on what we bring to it. -- Harold Bloom

I bring you my body, muscles flexing
to push me toward love, pull me from world's harm,
lift me to join, lower me to rest. Bring
you my mind and all it absorbs—alarms
of thought, will, reason awake unconscious,
carry me to opinion and desire,
all depending on memory, precious
Greek root word. I bring you my senses—fire
of the physical, scale of attachment
to earth, other bodies, their minds and hearts.
I bring you my spirit, utmost present
creating love, embryos, the great arts
raising our being to life beyond death,
swirled in endless conscious of the Great Breath.

NO WAY TO SAY GOODBYE

Feel this: nothing between my shoulders and
thighs but my heart and nuts clamped in a vise
tied with a Gordian knot. Sweaty hands
hurtling small cassette's forward and reverse
in eternal relay, hearing Leonard
Cohen over and over: *Hey, that's no*
way to say goodbye . . . a caveman retard
impotent to tears, hunched on Avenue
of Americas' curb, passion's discard
numb to spring sun and blossoms. I didn't
even want to drink. Just die. What's so hard
about life: instinct. Its ape hand senses
and snags will's last rung, refuses to let
go if we're lucky, and won't collect bets.

PARDON ME, PLEASE

Pardon me, please. I seem to write sonnets
each time I see you. This inspiration,
I suppose, springs forth as with most poets
confronted by beauty. Hesitation's
unhealthy for us. We respond with ease
to the appearing Muse, just as viewers
in museums praise Van Gogh's masterpiece
displayed before them, recognize its pure
and rare essence, like miners for gold who
suddenly stumble on a lone diamond,
or mountain-cave explorers finding blue
sky, and at cliff's edge uncharted ocean.
Poets don't seek out such amazing tides.
Truth is, the Muse flows forth when she decides.

CONSTIPATION

This hardened fear lodged deep in my bowel
bloats me with doubting, chronic inaction,
distorting my brow with distended scowl,
insane response to my heart's attraction
as you and your smile, nature's corona,
sweep past, sweet wisp of soft summer evening,
unaware my psyche's marooned on a
cramped island of shy despair. Your leaving
now will only extend my loin's fever.
Please, love, stay awhile. Make my pained body
a vessel of grace, grateful receiver
of your calming touch. Relieve my shoddy
diffidence with caress, helping me live
a lover's dream, your kiss my laxative.

I REALLY LIKE HOLDING YOU

I really like holding you, those precious
seconds. I really like how your soft eyes
glow on seeing me, how we're not cautious
moving to each other, as though our wise
angels have guided us through centuries
of renewed lives, always expecting brief
meetings, knowing our arms spread open, free
as sunflowers caressing light. Time, thief
of normal days, doesn't seem to count here
with you. Where shall we end up, do you feel?
I envision simple space, free from fear,
gazing at life's ageless art. A place real
as my bright couch, caressing, we alone
with old songs, like teens with the parents gone.

PARTICLES

S ince we are all particles of godlife,
since we all exercise within godbreath,
find our way and simply grow in godlight,
share intelligent energy past death,
since our collected cells can only see
our single cells flow through microscopic
invention we ourselves envision, we
ourselves create from other cells—topics
of our every thought, decision, action
and reaction—discover particles
smaller than our cells, great dancing fractions
as if life within life, and yet ourselves,
since all our cells share power through a kiss,
and kiss shares many forms, I write you this.

AIX-EN-PROVENCE

Look there to the east, love, how we still see
Montagne Sainte-Victoire as Cézanne saw
her, the way sunlit tinges of blue bleed
with pink and gray, pastel mask over raw
limestone. Let's sit under aqua awnings
of Les Deux Garçons, sip red Bandol as
he and Zola did till misty dawnings
long before their parting, lift each wine glass
and swear we two will last, solid as that
distant mountain, balanced as his bowing
bathers, at peace in our fluid abstract
setting, anonymous in our flowing
forms to any voyeur but God—artist
whose graceful brush allows us to exist.

SPRING TIDE

Sometimes you are sun, and so I circle
you in psychic pirouette, warmed by your glow
yet distant from explosion, miracle
in space and time. Sometimes you are moon, show
grace as you circle me, soft shadows of
your body impressing every seeing
eye's imagination, gazing above
at you reflecting your other being.
Sometimes you are both, aligning with me
in syzygy, your tidal forces, bold
as storms, igniting me, and my tides leap
up toward stars, toward dreams as constant and old
as Hipparchus who, from Rhodes' acropolis
smiled, first to predict our solar eclipses.

THE RESPONSIBILITY OF FEELING

For years I ran from it, not so sly fox
scurrying through gnarled forests, tainted lairs
housing lethal smiles, always fearing clocks,
their hackings timing my demise, those stares
from loved ones final as planets flooded
and lifeless there in clearings I shunned as
bats retreat from light, my scarred face hooded
from sight, till running fell to crawl, my last
gasp a kneeling rasp for help. I can't swear
just what happened next. I'm told how I slept
under a willow tree for days, nightmares
hurling howls from my parched mouth. Someone kept
feeding me sips of water. I awoke.
She smiled at me, then left. We never spoke.

POLISH TOWN SHARING MY ZIP CODE

Just two degrees separating today's
high and low here in Nowogard, too warm
for soft mist morphing to snow. Jadwiga
(named for the feminist miner, her arm
broken, then forehead blown off for striking
in the Seventeenth Century) giggles
as I study Hotel Oskar's lime-green
wall, quip I hunger for pie. She wiggles
her index, chides how I shouldn't make fun.
We pause at the granite monument: four
soldiers, straight and pointed as missiles, one
capped more like a bishop. Right after our
lake walk, we'll mazurka, sip Pompanskis,
then flirt over bigos and pierogi.

VALENTINE'S DAY

If you were here, I'd tell you how the priest
disobeyed cruel Claudius, marrying
lovers, though the emperor had released
no one from his law, its weight carrying
men to war. And the price the priest paid:
bones crushed by clubs; a blade-severed head.
But, oh, before then, how soft words he said
to the jailer's daughter--poems he read
her by candlelight--filled her with bright tears.
How hands touched through bars, making bodies flame.
How their vow, to never forget, for years
would allow her to live alone, their fame
leading lovers to share the final line
of his last, brief note: "From Your Valentine."

"HERE'S LOOKING AT YOU, KID"

In mystic airport fog, Bogie's talking
to Bergman. Curtiz and Edeson hold
him in close-up. I find myself flicking
the remote on *still*, pushing like some bold
producer up to the legend's face. "Shit,
Rick," I snap at the 26-inch screen,
"Cut the crap. You're smarter than the film script.
Grab Ilsa, Laszlo, Renault, Sam. You've seen
they all hold transit letters. Jump the plane,
soar to Lisbon and its nest of spies. Dance
under King Jose's statue. Laugh in rain,
Ilsa pressed to your chest. Yes, choose romance.
Let Victor win the war, fitting his name.
Let Louis slide. He understands the game.

"Leave the free French garrison for DeGaulle.
Sly your way to New York. Open up Rick's
Café Casablanca somewhere near Wall
Street, or in the Village. Let Ilsa pick
the apartment in Soho; let Sam play
on a Steinway. How many years do you
have left, anyway? Thirty? Forty, say?
Look at me! Roosevelt's lied, Truman too.
Ike will lie, Kennedy, Nixon, Clinton
will lie, and Bush will set Guinness records.
They don't care about us. Why stay bent on
sacrificing? Set your own peace accord.
Hold Ilsa as though the last day lurks near.
Kiss her. Whisper those words she longs to hear."

I LONELY AM

I lonely am you of thinking night this
when smile shadowed of moon from above shines
and hill this beyond village lights small kiss
echo like memory like wind of pines
through falling long glistens shoulders your hair
over and breasts as angel's hand your flow
wing-like my face blessed on warm feeling air
eyes my one your eyes as light heart aglow
as beating one let oh night not this fade
body before your my body burn grass
in soft as one lie we smiles our bright made
stars of angels heaven's like flight in pass
over they us calling voices follow
to only they lovers place the allow.

BY THE WAY

I've been thinking about you a lot: how
your eyes searched me quickly as we ended lunch at
Damgoode, your voice suggesting chow
after our vacations; then you amended
softly with . . . *if you want to* . . . I said *yes.*
A decided understatement. It's like
I photographed your stare: a look, I guess,
aroused by past torn promises, psychic
scars from hearing lies, perhaps. Of course, this
could just prove poet's fancy, or mirror
my own history of hope, care and loss.
I watched you leave, recalled how men adore
you. Prayed you'd find the happiness you seek.
Downstairs I learned you bought me lunch, you sneak.

DEEP LONELINESS

Perhaps today, bare winter trees screening
afternoon sun into bone-thin shadows—
lain like starved corpses across this winding
asphalt drive and still creek swelled with stuffed rows
of wet dead leaves—or perhaps Hillcrest's cold
streets with stripped Christmas trees tossed onto curbs
I studied as I walked here, let unfold
this feeling like my constant dream (disturbed
heart pounding, body falling, forever
falling through sphered black hole, endlessly deep
gorge of Great Evil's jaws). Or perhaps her
sad eyes—glowing like misty light—I keep
locked in my heart's vault, gem of memories,
reflect my soul. Perhaps it's all of these.

CEDAR WAXWING

This red doll's hand on secondary's pure
   tip—gray-silk feather suddenly turning
to fingers grafted from bright waxed sculpture—
provides the noun. Birds' streaked black masks yearning
for mystery and romance, high-pitched lilt
calling for all to *see*! Aggressive as
mobs, they flood—not in flocks—but swarms, yet build
nests via pairs, court with flower petals
and insects passed back and forth. Have you seen
them form a twig column for hard-to-reach
berries? Pass them beak to beak, assuring
each team member eats? Just how do they teach
that? See them sweep off in flight, my darling:
wings triangled and rapid, like starlings.

READING AMY

Love, I've read Amy Fusselman's memoir
fragment in NYT's "Lives" column, and
something's changed, like when oxygen and our
lungs live as one. She writes of human hands,
how they kill spirit and heal spirit. She
does this with simple gestures, phrases small
and powerful, like child's hand waving free
of fear, or palms pressed in prayer—silent call
to the Great All. She doesn't say this. I
do because of what she's said, her clear voice
urging me to answer. January
8, rainy morning. I welcome my choice
to keep playing Christmas carols, hearing
Julie Andrews. The blésséd angels sing.

YOUR HEALING HANDS

No, not the terminal section of bird
wing, nor ape's hind foot, crustacean's chela,
single flower group's banana cluster,
branched rootstock of ginger, not some yellow-
tan bunch of tobacco leaves, nor pointers
of clocks—all these terms referred to as hands—
these intricate human organs incurred
every day with grasps, shakes, high fives as grand
as winning, low fives as cool as wit—not
even these gestures, grace and gratitude
expressed in tactile sense, measure a jot,
or so it seems, to calm cure you exude
when you touch and hold my fingers in yours,
gently gripping bicep, rubbing shoulder.

HOW WIZARDS FALL IN
SLOWEST MOTION

When the wizard walked on water, flowing
over the falls, he must have felt like I
did holding you that day of my going
away. How heat rose as I watched your eyes
when you walked toward me, pushing close, your
voice
soft as an ancient chant: "I have to go."
Your arms enfolded me. I had no choice
but to kiss your cheek—gentle way to show
you how wizards fall in slowest motion
when overtaken by gravity, safe
in caress of mist, glorious ocean
of another's care, like embracing wave
responding to some distant shore's welcome,
or gliding clouds carrying angels home.

PICTURES AT AN EXHIBITION

They all are you. I stroll my mystic mind's gallery—
pen-and-inks, watercolors
matching your eyes to tones of spring. I find
fall sky of your iris changing contours
as I pass glowing close-up of goddess
face, arched eyebrow like a distant storm cloud
granted peace. Every critic must profess
your classic presence within each frame—proud
pressing jaw set free by graceful lips, gaze
demanding honesty. Then your wall-length
reclining portrait, pearl and sapphire haze
embracing your body, sharp bare-boned strength
of sense and symmetry. My poetry
honors your architecture's mystery.

KEEP DANCING, LOVE

Keep dancing, love, keep dancing. Don't let your
bitter wonder hold you back. Reward flows
from chancing motion—so soothsayers, pure
in their vision through crystal, seem to know,
predict as if decision and passion
both erupt from soul's one subduction zone,
pouring forth through blood, muscle, skeleton,
igniting limber leaps, closed position
marrying us to great music. Oh, hold
me as I hold you, welcoming our waltz,
lost in our embrace, inspired to risk bold
whirls and dips, mouths near gasping as we pause.
Your shy eyes glance away, and I recall
past lives in Renoir's *Bal à Bougival.*

LOVE SIMILES

I love you like I love the mirrored dome
of a faucet's single water droplet
clinging to my fingertip; flexing comb
of the captive cockatoo who sublets
the pet shop window's corner stall. I love
you like I love the smooth tinge of amber
curling along my Indian rug, lean
as a sleeping fawn; the solid hammer
of great Pujols' bat on a baseball, keen
as a thunderclap. Caress of a glove
holding back the snarling gnaw of winter;
the ballet grace of the greatest center
of all time: Jabbar and his soft skyhook.
I love you like you love to read a book.

MOUNTAIN THANKSGIVING

We've turkey on our table, love. Dressing
   and trimmings. Witness lantern light
dimming
as we hold hands, bow our heads in blessing,
share the meal. But this keeps my head swimming:
How you glow in lantern light, eyes dancing
fireflies of delight, celebrating guests'
every move, it seems, even my glancing
a glass off our wood floor. I should have guessed
it, your love flame swirling to bonfire through
our years. I see it in simplest ways: your
skilled fingers tending our garden—jeweler
etching diamonds. Then your easy smile, sure
I'll glow like moonlight, or blaze like dusk's sun,
when we lay as one after guests are gone.

HOW DEEPLY WE LOVE

Like our nurse's needle drawing rich blood,
capsuling it to test our chances; or
our surgeon's skilled scalpel saving our good
flesh while freeing our sockets of tumors,
gently resurrecting our blind eyes' sight;
or ancient torchbearers descending through
shafts, faithfully bringing lost miners light.
We constantly heal each other, love, true
to our senses, sharing our secret vaults
of fear and longing, faith and confusion,
doubt and delight. It brings us to this, caught
in a blessed realm of passion and reason,
an endless depth lifting our souls to soaring
with what must be angels, singing, adoring.

THE RAIN IS WRITING A POEM

Hear it telegraphing its metaphor,
love? Calling its falling an endless herd
of small ponies prancing (their hooves never
stampeding) across our yard. Every word
supports its rhythm, sends their dancing forms
forward, off across the countryside while
somehow remaining here with us. They're charms
in its meter, dear. We believe its mild
voice whispering, its predicting our near
season when soft gaits glancing off our roof
gently signal landing, resting reindeer
lightly stamping, offering perfect proof
a saint will soon enter our house—even
here where we see no snow—bringing heaven.

CHRISTMAS CANDLE

Oh, how close I move to this glowing white
flame, stretching, flickering like a searing
saber nearly singeing my brow. Its light,
symbol of world's salvation—appearing
a miracle floating on crimson wax
pool nearly cresting small tan wooden bowl—
suddenly softens, leans toward your relaxed
frame, love. Leans more, and I gaze into soul
of your candle eyes, their glowing white flames
singeing my frame, your candle smile calling
me to you, warm air caroling our names.
How close I move to you, our forms falling
as one, stretching, flickering like searing
sabers, world's salvation all endearing.

WINTER SOLSTICE

December 21st, near 6 pm,
you stand on Fifth Avenue, gaze immersed
in Bergdorf Goodman's vast "Compendium
of Curiosities." My mind forms verse,
not from etched, reflective reveries of
glowing glass throughout holiday windows,
but from watching you celebrate this trove
of art and artifacts. This eve bestows
winter solstice, love. All clocks mark this time,
though we'd never know now our sun stands still.
Snow clouds have rushed our night.
Their stout forms climb and mass,
covering dusk's light. Yet you fill
our space with stardust, praise crystal display
of unicorns. Your eyes chase chill away.

WIDENING CIRCLES

Rilke wondered if he were a falcon,
storm, or great song. Bill Yeats' second coming
complained his stirring bird couldn't hearken
the falconer. I swirl here, love, sturming
through fir tree branches, books, and banal talk,
flicking page corners to hold simple thought,
find hope within a phrase, breathlessly stalk
others' eyes to prove I'm alive. You caught
me on the building's ledge at Christmas, knew
my ill intent, filled my hand with yours, stood
with me, invited minuet, then true
pirouettes of joy. Our spinning made wood
boards shake, the room's walls swell, intense circles
sweeping wider, arms enclosing the world.

HYMNS YOU NEVER HEAR

My silent songs of praise seem to follow
your every move. I celebrate your hands,
delicate as rain, aligning brief rows
of biscuits in buttered pans, rainbow bands
of roses among our school of vases.
Love, I offer mute paeans when you smile
at seeing me, your eyes brilliant phases
of moonlight, your soft kiss my chamomile,
instant taste of peace. When I sense you feel
pain or sadness, my being intones chants
of hope, prayers for help, simply to reveal
how I may salve your suffering. I dance
within to rhythms of your breathing, your
heartbeat, your slightest touch my saintly cure.

A GREAT PRESENCE STIRS

With darkness surrounding us, love, we hold
one another like life preservers, drift
in ebony air as angels must, bold
as angels in our blessed mission. Now lift
each other, weightless in our altered state,
with such fragile care you'd think we'd shatter
if dropped or grasped with slightest force. We wait,
feel each other's breathing. Does it matter
how, years before, we warped treasured senses,
tossing each other's hearts in damp dungeons
only to watch our spirits escape? Yes.
Actions define our continuum. Once
we've returned, clawed, starved as our bodies are,
we see why angels once fought a great war.

YOU'RE CRYING, LOVE

You're crying, love. I can only listen
over my cell phone, feeling your stuttered
breath capture my breath, see your tears glisten
in imagined candlelight. You uttered
something about cherishing my poems,
words swirling around my head like ether,
too enshrined within your pain to see them
beyond you. Your eyes dance through odd-metered
lines, welcoming their window-framed shadows
each time like ghosts they appear before you,
slender spirits of script lying in snow.
You hang up, yet I feel soft residue
of your tears in my tears, fear somehow you'll
call me fool for crying. But I'm no fool.

TO FREE WHAT
WAITS WITHIN

I must welcome my senses, no longer
pretend I'm a lone brain floating in space,
acting as though isolation's stronger
than honest contact. Love, I've made my case
for avoiding life based on evidence
now dissolved to dust. Now my being must
welcome my whole body's startling movements,
your body's every reflex. It's not lust
I speak of, but facing realities
marking us as human, opening our
heat and light to join loving deities
who formed us, placing us this sacred hour
right here in our universe, facing each
other like stunned saints, heaven in our reach.

TO MAKE EACH HOUR HOLY

I will walk among my fellows, hold their
hands and study their eyes. That's all I need
to do. If God exists, surely it's where
touch and sight meld within us, spirit's seed
nourished by heat and light flowing from nerves
to brain, to heart, to gut and groin. We
know our universe through senses, deserve
our sixth sense leading us to faith. We're free
to choose whether to live, to recognize
heartbeat and breath as gifts opening our minds
to all that's possible. Free to despise
and despair should we choose fear, even find
insanity safer than love. But I
find you, love, by seeking with hand and eye.

I WRITE THIS POEM

I write this poem to beauty. I write
this poem to grace. I write this poem
to the silent instance between lark's flight
and cricket's call as shadows fall—slow hymns
to honor sun's memory through Allsopp's
woods. Tell me only good comes from our soft
words wandering like small children through stops
and starts along this wonderland, this loft
of gentle space between us, within us.
Tell me with your silence you understand when
I stare as if surrounded by stardust
turning this low-lighted room to heaven.
I write this poem to show sacred worth
of us here at ease, like no place on earth.

ABOUT THE POET

Roger Armbrust served as national news editor of NYC's *Back Stage* magazine, taught writing at NYU, edited books on national social issues, and fathered a remarkable artist. He currently serves as co-curator of the online journal *The Clyde Fitch Report: The nexus of arts and politics*. His other books of poetry include *How to Survive* and *The Aesthetic Astronaut*.